Contents

Fairy tale: 'Jack and the Beanstalk'

From 'Jack and the Beanstalk' by Vivian French

Jack's mother took in other people's washing to make a little money, but as she got older she found this harder and harder. Jack was no help to her. He dropped the washing and lost the pegs and forgot to look to see if it was raining. He was much too busy sitting on the doorstep singing 'Dee-dah diddle-di-dee'.

At last there was no money left at all.

'Jack!' said his mother, and there were tears in her eyes. 'Jack! You must take poor Daisy to market and sell her. Sell her for as much money as you can, for we have nothing left.'

Get started

Copy the sentences and complete them using words from the story.

1. Jack's mother took in other people's _____ to make a little _____ .

2. As she got older she found this _____ and _____ .

3. At last there was no _____ left at _____ .

4. Jack had to take poor Daisy to _____ and _____ her.

Try these

Ask a teacher for help with any words in the story you do not know. Write a sentence to answer each question.

1. What was Jack singing?

2. Why did Jack's mother tell him to sell Daisy?

3. Why do you think Jack's mother had tears in her eyes?

4. Who do you think Daisy is?

Now try these

1. What is Jack like? Write a sentence.

2. Draw a picture of Jack going to the market. Add a sentence to show what Jack is thinking.

Traditional tale: 'Jamil's Clever Cat'

From 'Jamil's Clever Cat' by Fiona French, with Nick Newby

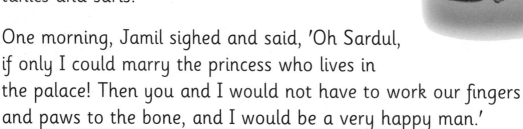

Jamil the weaver lived on the poor side of town. He had a cat called Sardul, a very clever cat. Each night, while Jamil was asleep, Sardul wove material for his master to make into tunics and saris.

One morning, Jamil sighed and said, 'Oh Sardul, if only I could marry the princess who lives in the palace! Then you and I would not have to work our fingers and paws to the bone, and I would be a very happy man.'

Sardul thought for a minute. Then he said, 'Give me the best waistcoat and the most beautiful sari we have made, Master, and I can make your dream come true.'

Get started

Copy the sentences and complete them using words from the story.

1. Jamil the weaver lived on the _____ side of _____ .

2. He had a _____ called Sardul.

3. Sardul wove _____ for his master to make into _____ and saris.

Try these

Ask a teacher for help with any words in the story you do not know. Write a sentence to answer each question.

1. What did Sardul do at night?

2. What did Jamil do with the material Sardul wove?

3. Why did Jamil want to marry the princess?

4. Why was Jamil lucky to have Sardul?

Now try these

1. What do you think Sardol's plan might be? Make notes about his plan.

2. Draw a picture of Jamil and Sardul meeting the princess. Add a sentence to show what the princess is thinking.

Contemporary tale: 'Tom's Sausage Lion'

From 'Tom's Sausage Lion' by Michael Morpurgo

It was Christmas Eve when Tom first saw the lion. His mother had sent him out to fetch the logs, and there was a lion padding through the orchard with a string of sausages hanging from its mouth. Tom ran back inside the house to tell them, but his father just laughed and his mother said he must have been imagining things. He told them and he told them, but they wouldn't even come out to look.

'But it's true,' Tom shouted. 'It was a real lion, I know it was.'

'Perhaps it just looked like a lion,' said his mother. 'After all, it is getting dark outside, isn't it, dear?'

Get started

Copy the sentences and complete them using words from the story.

1. It was Christmas Eve when _____ first saw the _____ .

2. His mother had sent him _____ to fetch the _____ .

3. There was lion padding through the _____ with a string of _____ hanging from its mouth.

Try these

Ask a teacher for help with any words in the story you do not know. Write a sentence to answer each question.

1. What day was it?

2. Why had Tom gone out?

3. Why do you think his father and mother wouldn't go and look?

4. Why do you think Tom shouted?

Now try these

1. Do you think there really was a lion? Why do you think this? Write one or two sentences.

2. Draw a picture of the moment Tom first sees the lion. Add a sentence to show what he is thinking.

Classic poetry: 'Some One'

Someone came knocking
At my wee, small door;
Some one came knocking,
I'm sure-sure-sure;
I listened, I opened,
I looked to left and right,
But nought there was a-stirring

In the still dark night;
Only the busy beetle
Tap-tapping in the wall,
Only from the forest
The screech-owl's call,
Only the cricket whistling
While the dewdrops fall,
So I know not who came knocking,
At all, at all, at all.

Walter de la Mare

Get started

Copy the lines and complete them using words from the poem.

1. Someone came _____ At my wee, small _____ ;

2. I listened, I opened, I looked to _____ and _____ ,

3. Only the busy _____ Tap-tapping in the _____ ,

4. Only the cricket _____ While the _____ fall,

Try these

Ask a teacher for help with any words in the poem you do not know. Write a sentence to answer each question.

1. What was tapping in the wall?

2. What was calling in the forest?

3. Why did the speaker of the poem open the door?

4. How do you think the speaker of the poem feels? Why do you think this?

Now try these

1. Rhyming words are words that sound like each other. The words 'door' and 'sure' are rhyming words in this poem. Find and write the other rhyming words in the poem. Then add other words that sound like them.

2. Draw a picture of the speaker of the poem looking out of the little door. What details from the poem can you include in the picture? Add a sentence to show what the speaker is thinking.

Classic poetry : 'Who's There?'

Knock, knock!

Who's there?
cried the spider.
Stand and wait!
But she knew by the
gentle tweak of the web
it was her mate.

Knock, knock!
Who's there?
cried the spider.
Call your name!
But she knew by the
soft tap-tap on the silk
her spiderlings came.

Knock, knock!
Who's there?
cried the spider.
Who goes by?
But she knew by the
shaking of her net
it was the fly.

Judith Nicholls

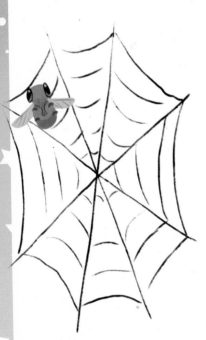

Get started

Copy the lines and complete them using words from the poem.

1. Knock, knock! *Who's* _____ ? cried the _____ .

2. But she knew by the gentle _____ of the web it has her _____ .

3. But she knew by the of her net it was the _____ .

Try these

Write a sentence to answer each question about the poem.

1. Who gave a 'soft tap-tap' on the silk?

2. How did the fly move the spider's net?

3. What are the rhyming words in the poem?

Now try these

1. Note down one idea for a different creature that touches the spider's web. Describe a new way this creature could touch it, to let the spider know what it is.

2. Draw and label a picture of the spider on her web, with one of her three visitors.

Word play: 'Eletelephony'

Once there was an elephant,
Who tried to use the telephant –
No! No! I mean an elephone
Who tried to use the telephone –
(Dear me! I am not certain quite
That even now I've got it right.)

Howe'er it was, he got his trunk
Entangled in the telephunk;
The more he tried to get it free,
The louder buzzed the telephee –
(I fear I'd better drop the song
Of elephop and telephong!)

Laura E. Richards

Get started

Copy the lines and complete them using words from the poem.

1. Once there was an _____ , Who tried to use the _____ –

2. No! No! I mean an elephone Who tried to _____ the _____ –

3. Dear me! I am not certain quite That _____ now I've got it _____.

Try these

Ask a teacher for help with any words in the poem you do not know. Write a sentence to answer each question about the poem.

1. What was the elephant really trying to do?

2. What noise did the telephone make?

3. What problem did the elephant really have with his trunk?

4. What are the funny nonsense words in the poem?

Now try these

1. Explain why the words 'elephant' and 'telephone' can be muddled up.

2. Draw a picture of the elephant trying to use the telephone. Label the picture using all the nonsense words in the poem to show what the poet really meant by these words.

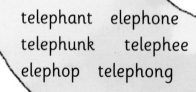

telephant   elephone
telephunk   telephee
elephop   telephong

Instructions: Be a snake charmer

Experiment with static electricity in this charming activity.

1. Put a plate on a piece of tissue paper and draw around it. Cut out the circle. Draw a spiral snake inside it, like this.

2. To decorate your snake, use felt-tip pens to draw a zigzag pattern and eyes. Then cut along the spiral.

3. Rub a plastic ruler fairly hard and fast for half a minute with a scarf or sweater made of wool.

4. Then touch the snake's head with your ruler. Slowly lift the ruler. The snake should uncoil and rise up.

What's going on?

When the wool is rubbed against the plastic ruler, it causes particles too small to see to pass from the wool to the ruler. These extra particles on the ruler cause a build-up of static electricity. The static pulls on the tissue paper. The tissue paper is so light that the static on the ruler is strong enough to lift it.

Get started

Copy the sentences and complete them using words from the instructions.

1. Experiment with static _____ in this _____ activity.

2. Put a plate on a piece of _____ paper and draw _____ it.

3. To decorate your snake, use felt-tip pens to draw a _____ pattern and _____ .

Try these

Ask a teacher for help with any words in the instructions you do not know. Write a sentence to answer each question.

1. What is the first thing you have to do?

2. What should you draw with felt-tip pens?

3. How do the pictures of the snake and ruler help?

Now try these

1. Make a list of the items you need to do this activity.

2. Draw and label a diagram that could help someone to follow instruction 4.

Explanations: 'Seeing the world'

From 'Your Senses' by Sally Morgan

We need light to see. Light enters your eye through your pupil, the black spot in the middle of your eye. When the light is dim, your pupil is large, so that lots of light can enter. But when the light is bright, your pupil is small to stop too much light getting in and damaging your eye.

Light passes through your pupil and falls on the back of your eye, where information is sent to your brain. Your brain uses the information to build a picture of what you see.

front of eye

light

pupil

Light falls on the back of your eye and a message is sent to your brain.

The message travels along your optic nerve to your brain.

Get started

Copy the sentences and complete them using words from the explanation.

1. Light enters your eye through your _____ , the black spot in the _____ of your eye.

2. When the light is dim, your pupil is _____ , so that lots of _____ can enter.

3. Light passes through your pupil and falls on the _____ of your eye, where information is sent to your _____ .

Try these

Ask a teacher for help with any words in the explanation you do not know. Write one or two sentences to answer each question.

1. Why do people need light?

2. In this explanation, what is a pupil?

3. Does your eye build up a picture of what you see? If not, what does?

4. How would your pupils change if you went from a dark room into bright sunlight?

Now try these

1. In your own words, explain what happens to the light when it enters your eye.

2. Draw and label a picture of light entering someone's eye. Use arrows to show the light. Use the explanation text to find the details.

Non-chronological report

What is a gerbil?

Gerbils are small, mouse-like animals with hairy tails and strong back legs. They are clean and fun-loving, and make excellent pets.

Appearance

Gerbils are about 10 cm (4 in.) tall – larger than a mouse, but smaller than a rat.

Desert diggers

Wild gerbils and their relatives come from desert regions. They live in groups called colonies, inside huge networks of tunnels that they dig in the sand.

Need to gnaw

Like rats and hamsters, gerbils are rodents. These are animals with two pairs of strong front teeth for gnawing. The name 'gerbil' comes from the Arabic word 'jarbou', meaning 'rodent'.

Get started

Copy the sentences and complete them using words from the report.

1. Gerbils are small, mouse-like animals with _____ tails and _____ back legs.

2. Gerbils are about 10 cm (4 in.) tall – larger than a _____ , but a smaller than a _____ .

Try these

Ask a teacher for help with any words in the report you do not know. Write one or two sentences to answer each question.

1. How could you tell the difference between a gerbil and a mouse?

2. In which parts of the world do wild gerbils live?

3. Why does the writer think that a gerbil would make a good pet?

4. What are the sub-headings in this report? Why are they used?

Now try these

1. If you wanted to get a gerbil as a pet, what other information might you like to know? Write at least three questions that you could ask.

2. Draw and label a picture of a gerbil. Use the report to find the details. Write three other facts from the report about the gerbil.